MUTING
THE GUITAR
By David Brewster

ISBN 978-1-57424-236-2
SAN 683-8022

Cover by James Creative Group

Introduction

Chapter 1 – *The Sound Of Silence*

Chapter 2 – *Frethand Muting Techniques*
CD Tracks 1-38

Chapter 3 – *Pickhand Muting Techniques*
CD Tracks 39-49

Chapter 4 – *Combination Muting Techniques*
CD Tracks 50-70

Legato Phrasing And Muting

Introduction

The guitar is one of the most challenging musical instruments to learn and can be unforgiving when executing chords, scales, and various playing techniques cleanly. Unlike other instruments, such as the piano, the guitar requires the user to manipulate and mute the strings manually, which can prove to be very difficult from the beginning.

For many guitarists the abundance of noise, uncontrolled strings ringing, and the various "bleeps" and "clicks" that can occur while playing can become extremely frustrating and annoying. This is why various muting techniques should be explored to ensure a "clean" sounding performance.

The muting technique you'll ultimately need to use will depend on what you're performing, as you might need to utilize more than one muting style at the same time during a song or musical exercise. The guitar is a very "hands-on" instrument, so learning how to efficiently mute anything that you will perform from this day forward is very important.

Techniques for muting the guitar strings have been refined for a very long time, "passed around" from one musical style and guitarist to another. From the palm muting techniques refined by legendary Blues, Rock, and Country guitarists, to the frethand muting technique used when performing octaves (notably developed and refined by Jazz guitar giant Wes Montgomery), the guitar is truly a unique and diversely complicated instrument.

This book was created to educate guitarists with the vast and commonly overlooked techniques of string muting for the guitar. Within these pages (and accompanying audio CD) there are three main types of muting shown and discussed, muting with the frethand (type 1) and the pickhand (type 2). The last chapter of this book demonstrates a few playing situations where both hands work together to dampen and mute the strings (type 3).

Once you have practiced these muting concepts, you should incorporate the examples shown in this book and any variations of these muting techniques into your everyday playing as soon as possible.

Special Thanks

To Mom & Dann, Dad, Deb (and the boys), Danielle & Alyssa McCrary,
Emily Endress, Ron at Centerstream, Jeff at Hal Leonard, Susan at Cherry Lane,
Dave Storey at Dava Picks, and to all my students (past and present).

About The Author

David Brewster is an honors graduate from the Atlanta Institute of Music.
He has books available through Centerstream, Hal Leonard, and Cherry Lane.
For more information and to hear samples of his music visit:
www.myspace.com/brewhamusicinc

Chapter 1 – *The Sound of Silence*

Before learning how to adapt muting techniques into your playing, make sure your equipment is ready for the task at hand. Unfortunately, many guitarists neglect their instrument (and other essential equipment) to the point where it affects the overall playability and function.

Follow these simple guidelines to ensure your equipment is working properly and ready for action.

Basic Guitar Care

The guitar (electric or acoustic) can create many noises and "pops" when it has been neglected. Old strings, improper maintenance, and faulty electrical wiring can cause excessive noise when amplified.

1. Change your strings regularly!
2. Clean your guitar regularly, including the fretboard & frets.
3. Take your guitar to a technician and have a "tune-up", where the truss rod and playing "action" are adjusted. This should be done at least once a year.
4. Have your intonation set (intonation is the fine-tuning of a guitar). Be sure to have your intonation adjusted by someone with experience.
5. Check your volume and tone potentiometers (knobs) for noise when you roll them around while amplified. If can you hear a scratching sound when you manipulate the volume or tone controls on your guitar, they might need contact cleaning or a replacement.
6. Make sure your guitar is wired, grounded, and shielded correctly. Visit a repair shop or music store and have your guitar looked over by a qualified technician.

Basic Amplifier Care

Once your guitar is ready, take a close look at your amplifier to be sure that everything is working properly.

1. If your amplifier has tubes, have them checked regularly.
2. Be sure that your input jacks, volume and tone potentiometers (knobs) are clean and don't need to be replaced or cleaned.
3. If you normally practice or perform at loud volume levels - check your speaker(s) for replacement regularly. (You'd be surprised how many players don't realize they have a faulty or blown speaker in their amp)
4. If you are using a head and cabinet set-up, make sure the Ohm reading for the head and cabinet are compatible.

It is recommended to have an amplifier checked over by a technician when faced with an annoying hum or a strange noise. A qualified repairperson can evaluate what is causing the noise and repair the amplifier by cleaning or replacing the faulty components to help remedy a noisy amp.

Additional Equipment Care

Once you're certain that your guitar and amplifier are working correctly, identify a few additional components that might generate noise in your signal.

1. Be sure the cables that you're using work properly. If you're in doubt, use a cable tester, which can usually be found in music stores or repair shops.
2. If you're using foot pedals or a pedalboard, be sure to use the correct adaptors and/or fresh batteries with any extraneous gear that might create additional noise in your signal.
3. Florescent lighting, computer and television monitors, cell phones, radio waves, and various other types of "invisible" technology can wreak havoc for amplified guitarists. If you're suffering from an annoying "hum" coming from your amplified guitar, there are countless variables that may be causing the noise.

*Remember - Make sure all of your equipment is functioning properly and extra noises from your equipment are kept to a minimum before practicing or playing guitar amplified. By doing this, you'll know if it's you or your equipment that is adding additional noise when playing or performing.

From Zero to Hero - *Using The Volume Knob*

Once you have checked over your equipment, you should discover (or re-discover) the most reliable way of silencing an amplified guitar, as many guitarists forget they have an ally in the fight against uncontrollable noises, the very-useful volume knob.

The easiest way to silence an amplified guitar is by rolling off the volume knob when not playing. Once you're finished playing through a song or musical exercise, make it a habit to roll off the volume, preventing any unwanted sounds or noises that could occur from being amplified.

It's common courtesy to turn the volume down on a guitar when handing it to someone while it's plugged in. Anytime you are playing or doing something with the guitar that you don't want others to hear, roll the volume knob to zero.

Carefully watch a professional guitarist perform live and you'll notice they will change the settings of their volume, tone, and pickup selection to help attain a certain quality of sound and timbre, in addition to silencing their instrument using a volume knob or volume pedal.

Many professional guitarists use volume pedals or channel switching during concerts to give their live instruments an automatic "kill switch". This allows them to silence their instrument instantly and can noticeably occur between the songs of a set or when switching to a different guitar.

Chapter 2 – *Frethand Muting Techniques*

Learning to mute the strings using the frethand fingers is essential for a number of different playing situations on the guitar. String "scratching", thumb muting, power chord strumming, performing octaves, string "raking", and other playing techniques directly involve frethand muting in some form.

"Fretboard Smother" Technique

The first muting technique you should learn involves placing the frethand fingers lightly across the six strings of the guitar, which will prevent the strings from sounding when they are strummed or plucked.

You should use a light touch and be cautious not to accidentally perform natural harmonics when applying the "fretboard smother" technique.

This is a fail-safe way of controlling the strings of the guitar. Many popular songs and musical styles feature guitarists using this form of string muting to control the strings.

Study this photo to learn the hand position for the "fretboard smother" technique, practice this technique giving you the ability to stop all the strings from sounding or ringing instantly.

Try this exercise (Ex.1), which will test how efficient you are at muting all of the strings on the guitar. As you play through this exercise, the only audible sound should be the dampened strings when picking from string to string.

Example 1 - "Fretboard Smother" Exercise CD 1

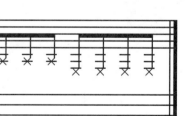

This example (Ex.1) is a very good picking exercise, which will improve string-to-string picking coordination. You should practice this exercise using downstrokes only at first, and then incorporate strict alternate picking (down-up-down-up).

To continue, mute the strings using the "fretboard smother" technique and strum this straight eighth-note rhythm (Ex.2).

Example 2 - Strumming The "Fretboard Smother" CD 2

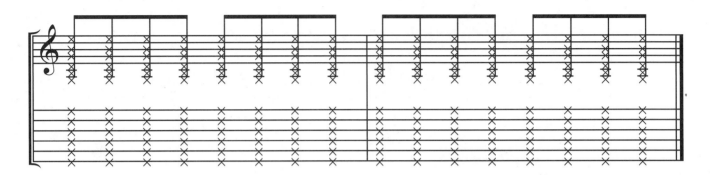

Guitar legend Jimi Hendrix used this muting technique in some of his most famous songs such as 'Voodoo Chile (Slight Return)' and the immortal live cut from Band Of Gypsys, 'Machine Gun'.

Once you're comfortable using the "fretboard smother" technique, incorporate a few chords to make things more interesting and musical. The first chord you should mute using the "fretboard smother" technique is a common E9 chord shape (Ex.3).

Example 3 - E9 Chord CD 3

Once the chord is comfortably fretted and performed on the guitar, lightly lift your fingers and mute the strings while retaining the E9 chord shape using the "fretboard smother" muting technique. The frethand fingers should only touch the strings hard enough to prevent them from ringing or sounding.

Play this muted rhythm using the "fretboard smother" muting technique and the E9 chord (Ex.4), further developing your "smothering" technique.

Example 4 - E9 "Frethand Smother" Rhythm #1  CD 4

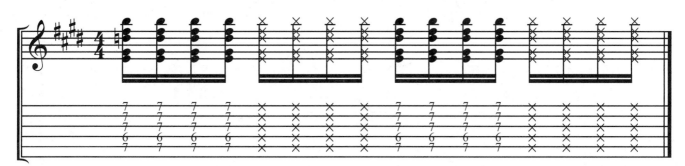

This muting technique is also known as "scratching" to most Funk and Rock guitarists.

Practice this strumming and muting exercise with the E9 chord (Ex.5). This type of muting can be found anywhere in Funk and Rock music, from James Brown and Parliament to the Red Hot Chili Peppers and Lenny Kravitz.

Example 5 - E9 "Frethand Smother" Rhythm #2 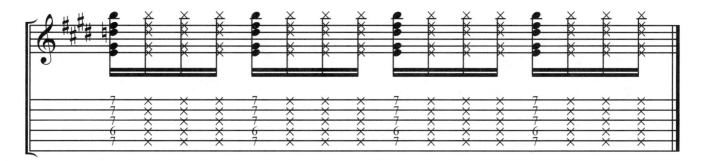 CD 5

The next example (Ex.6) is a common Funk rhythm using E9 and the neighboring E13 chord. The high C# of the E13 chord should be fretted using the pinky (4th) finger, simply remove it to return to the E9 chord.

Example 6 - "Smothered" Funk Rhythm Using E9 And E13 CD 6

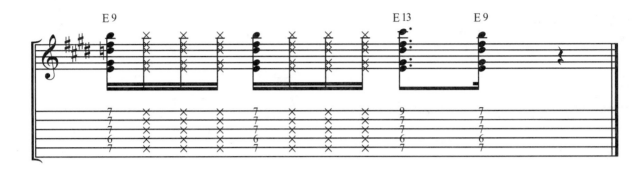

Here is a continuation of this muting style featuring a chord slide at the beginning of the riff (Ex.7). This type of rhythm is very common and Funk guitar masters such as Jimmy Nolen (James Brown) and Nile Rodgers (Chic), who both used this type of muted phrasing.

Example 7 - Variation Of Ex.6 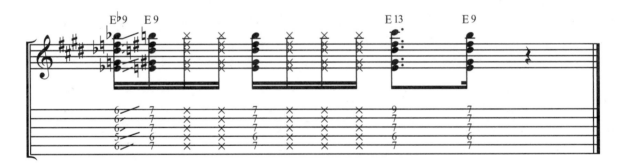 CD 7

If you're unfamiliar using the E9 and E13 together in a progression, practice both of these chord shapes until they're comfortable to play and executed cleanly.

The proper "feel" the frethand fingers should have when applying the "fretboard smother" technique falls somewhere between fretting notes regularly and performing natural harmonics on the guitar. If you're producing harmonics, relocate the fret position (whenever possible) or rearrange the frethand fingers to eliminate harmonic overtones.

Frethand "Smothered" Power Chords

Once you're comfortable muting the strings simultaneously using the "fretboard smother" and you've practiced the technique using ninth chords, you should practice using this muting technique with traditional power chords.

To begin, study the photo below demonstrating the proper frethand placement for muting an E5 power chord in seventh position with an 'A' string root (Ex.8).

Example 8 - E5 "Fretboard Smother" CD 8

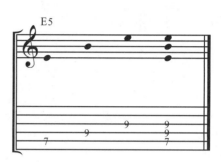

Notice in the previous photo that the underside of your third finger should lightly lie across the 'B' and high 'E' strings, while the tip of the index finger should lightly touch the side of the low 'E' string, properly muting the unused strings of this chord.

To give the power chord "fretboard smother" technique an authentic Rock sound, play around with this power chord riff (Ex.9), reminiscent of many Classic Rock songs such as 'China Grove' by the Doobie Brothers and 'More Than A Feeling' by Boston.

Example 9 - Muted Classic Rock Rhythm CD 9

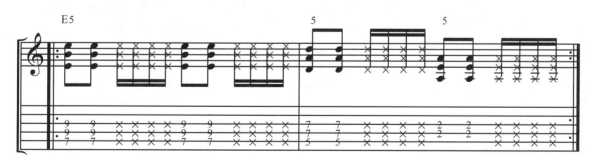

If you're playing a power chord with a root on the low 'E' string, mute as shown in the photo for this B5 power chord in the 7th position (Ex.10).

Example 10 - B5 "Fretboard Smother"   CD 10

Notice in the photo that the underside of the index and ring fingers are dampening the unused strings for this chord shape (Ex.10), properly muting the 'G', 'B', and high 'E' strings.

Play around with this Rock rhythm using the B5 power chord shape (Ex.11), complete with a root movement from the low 'E' to the 'A' string.

Example 11 - Muted Rock Rhythm   CD 11

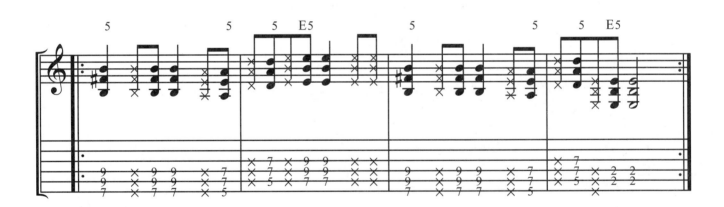

To give this muting technique an Alternative Rock twist, play around with this power chord riff (Ex.12), using the same the muting style found in many Alternative Rock hits such as 'Smells Like Teen Sprit' by Nirvana and 'Bulls On Parade' by Rage Against The Machine.

Example 12 - Muted Alternative Rock Rhythm CD 12

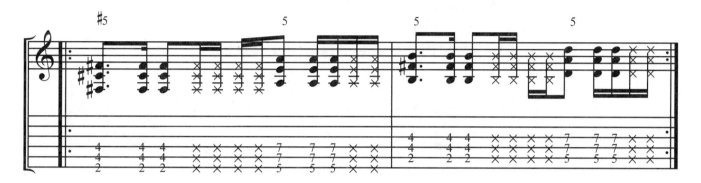

"Smothered" Reggae/Ska Muting

The next example (Ex.13) features the "fretboard smother" muting technique in a radically different musical setting. Play around with this Reggae styled strumming pattern and be sure to properly mute unwanted strings between the chord "hits".

Example 13 - Reggae "Smothered" Muting CD 13

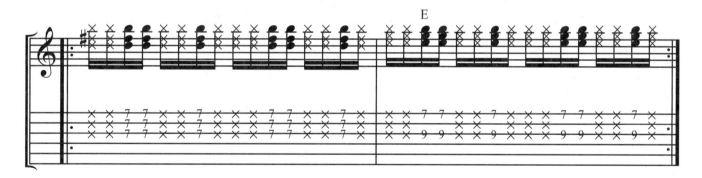

This example is similar to the muting style used in classic Reggae songs by artists such as Bob Marley and Peter Tosh.

You should notice that this example (Ex.13) uses different strings than the previous examples, so use a small strumming stoke and carefully position the frethand fingers to fret the chord parts when they are sounded, then dampen the strings when the muted sections are strummed.

It normally takes a considerable amount of time and patient practice before this muting technique becomes second nature and comfortable for the user. Take your time and be sure to listen to what you're playing with a critical ear, as you should be certain that unwanted strings and noises are not present when performing rhythms and riffs such as this.

For another example of using the "fretboard smother" technique, try this common Ska-Punk styled rhythm (Ex.14), commonly used by groups such as No Doubt, Sublime, Rancid, and The Mighty Mighty Bosstones.

Example 14 - Ska/Punk "Smothered" Muting   CD 14

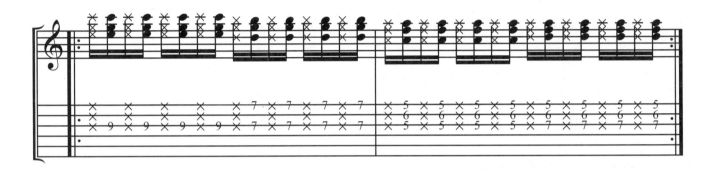

This example (Ex.14) features a quick transition between the muted and fretted strums with each chord. Be sure to practice this example slowly until you're comfortable muting in this manner. Listen to some of your favorite songs and musical groups to see if you hear this style of muting in their music.

Muting With The Frethand Thumb

You may have already noticed that many guitarists commonly use their frethand thumb to dampen or mute the low 'E' string while playing. This is intentional, as muting the strings with the tip of the frethand thumb has been around for a very long time.

To clearly see how to use the frethand thumb to mute the low 'E' string, strum through this common Asus2 chord (Ex.15).

Example 15 - Asus2 Chord   CD 15

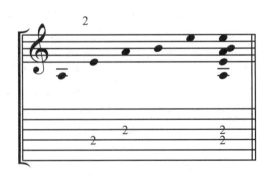

Strum through the Asus2 chord a few times using downstrokes and upstrokes to ensure that the frethand thumb is properly muting.

Try the next example (Ex.16), featuring the Asus2 chord shape shown in Ex.15, but it's moved to various locations along the guitar neck, creating an array of interesting chords.

Example 16 - Asus2 Chord Variations   CD 16

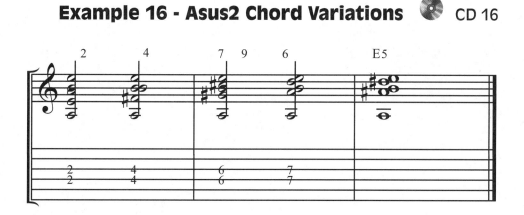

Continue using the thumb to mute unwanted strings for different chord shapes, such as this D Major chord in open position (Ex.17). Specifically the frethand thumb should mute the low 'E' and 'A' strings, using a common "thumb wrap" over the side of the fingerboard.

Example 17 - D Major "Thumb Wrap"   CD 17

Although the "thumb wrap" technique requires an extended reach over the side of the fingerboard, it allows to properly mute unwanted strings so you may strum this chord with reckless abandon, without the fear of sounding an unwanted string.

Once you've played through this example (Ex.17), continue to explore this style of muting by using the frethand thumb to mute other open position Major and Minor chords. If the chord requires five or fewer strings, such as A Minor or C Major, rest the side of the thumb along the low 'E' string to effectively mute the unused string.

For a slight twist on this technique, try fretting the second fret on the low 'E' string with the thumb while muting the 'A' string, a proper thumb mute for this common D/F# chord (Ex.18).

Example 18 - D/F# "Fretted Thumb Wrap" CD 18

Play around with this common chord progression, normally found in acoustic guitar music, featuring the D/F# chord shape mixed with common G and E Major chords (Ex.19).

Example 19 - "Thumb Wrap" Strumming Exercise CD 19

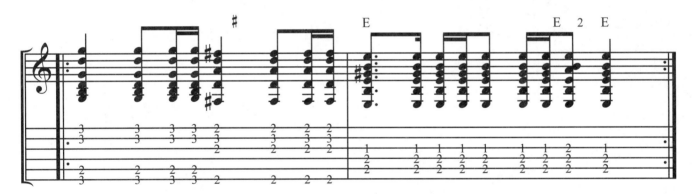

Making smooth transitions when playing open position chord progressions is a common playing situation found in numerous songs, from Folk and Country to Hard Rock and Pop. Many beginning and intermediate guitarists seem to have trouble keeping things muted and quiet when performing these chord changes, and using some clever dampening techniques from the frethand fingers is your ultimate goal here.

Jimi Hendrix used his thumb for muting and fretting while playing on many of his famous recordings. Classics such as 'Little Wing', 'Wind Cries Mary', and 'Castles Made Of Sand' feature Hendrix using his noticeably large thumb for muting and fretting notes along the low 'E' string and 'A' strings.

Play this common Hendrix G9 shape (Ex.20), which was featured during the intro of 'Castles Made Of Sand' and 'Little Wing'. Use the frethand thumb for fretting the third fret on the low 'E' string while muting the open 'A' string simultaneously.

Example 20 - G9 "Hendrix" "Fretted Thumb Wrap" CD 20

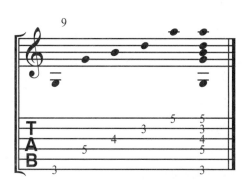

Play around with this Hendrix inspired G9 chord shift (Ex.21). Once you're able to play it cleanly, continue to shift this chord around the fingerboard to see what sounds you can create.

Example 21 - Hendrix Inspired 9th Chord Moves CD 21

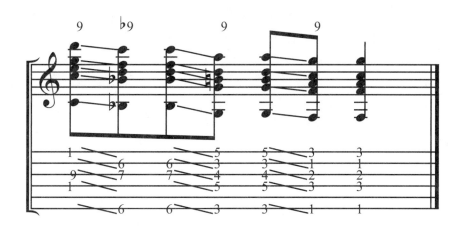

Since we are already on the subject of Jimi Hendrix, play around with this D7#9 voicing (Ex.22), which has been nicknamed the "Hendrix" chord and featured in classic songs such as 'Purple Haze' and 'Spanish Castle Magic'.

Example 22 - Muting The D7#9 ("The Hendrix Chord") CD 22

Notice that you'll need to mute the low 'E' string with the frethand thumb, while muting the high 'E' string using your fourth (pinky) finger for this 7#9 chord fingering.

Practice muting the "Hendrix" chord using this riff idea (Ex.23).

Example 23 - D7#9 Muted Riff CD 23

Frethand Thumb/Finger Muting Combinations

Now that you're accustomed to using the frethand thumb to mute the strings, you should learn how to use a combination of the thumb and unused frethand fingers. This will insure that you'll successfully mute the strings of the guitar when playing various chords, octaves, scales, and single note riffs.

It may seem like a daunting task, not only will you have to position your fingers for the notes and sounds that you actually want to produce, you'll also have to strategically position both hands wherever necessary to properly mute the unwanted strings. Practicing muting technique can become tedious, but it is well worth the effort, helping you sound more refined and professional.

To explore frethand combination muting, play through this simple variation of an open position G Major chord (Ex.24), which will yield a G5 power chord. This chord is commonly found in the music of AC/DC, Led Zeppelin, Van Halen, and countless Classic Rock legends.

Example 24 - G Major/Chord And Muted G5 Variation CD 24

 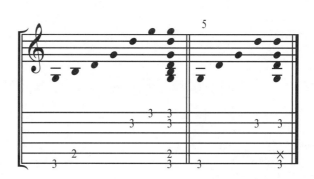

The specific muting technique that should be used with chords like these involves using two frethand fingers to mute the strings, a combination of the frethand middle and third (ring) fingers. Mute the A string with the underside of the middle finger, while using the underside of the third finger on the high 'E' string, similar to the technique that was used with the "Hendrix chord" (Ex.22).

Try another open position power chord using a muting technique similar to Example 22, the common D5/A (Ex.25). Mute the low 'E' string with the frethand thumb while using the middle finger to mute the high 'E' string.

Example 25 - D5/A Power Chord  CD 25

This A5 power chord (Ex.26) involves using the frethand thumb to mute the low 'E' string, while muting the 'B' and high 'E' strings with the underside of the index finger, the same finger that is barring the second fret of the 'D' and 'G' strings. Guitar legend Eddie Van Halen commonly uses this chord shape and muting technique.

Example 26 - A5 Power Chord  CD 26

Once you are comfortable muting these three open position power chords, play through this Rock riff (Ex.27), putting this muting technique to the ultimate test, using A5, D5, E5, and G5 power chords.

Example 27 - Open Position Muted Power Chord Example CD 27

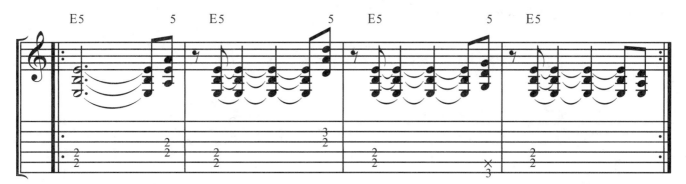

This example (Ex.27), is very similar to rhythms and riffs played by Hard Rock veterans AC/DC, who refined this type of power chord play during the 1970s. Many Rock guitarists took a cue from Angus and Malcolm Young (the guitarists in AC/DC) and learned how to mute power chords riffs such as this from them, including classic songs such as 'Back In Black', 'Dirty Deeds Done Dirt Cheap', and 'Highway To Hell'.

Frethand Octave Muting

Octaves have turned up in every imaginable musical genre, yet very little has been demonstrated on how to mute and perform them on the guitar, until now. An octave is the distance between two notes that are 12 half-steps apart. This "chord" could be thought of as a diad (a two-note chord), consisting of two notes with identical note names, but different pitches.

Performing octave shapes on the guitar presents a common noise problem for most guitarists, as it's very easy to accidentally hit unwanted strings, especially if the octave shapes move to different sets of strings or shift to different areas on the fretboard.

To begin, play this basic E octave found at the 7th position using the 'A' and 'G' strings (Ex.28). Try strumming it with your pick or with the side of your pickhand thumb (ala Wes Montgomery).

Example 28 - E Octave Shape CD 28

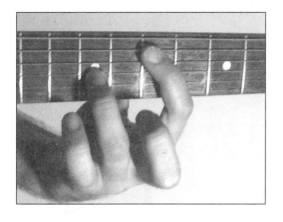

The muting secret behind playing an octave lies in the proper finger placement when holding down the shape. The index and third fingers should lightly lie across the strings that aren't being used and the tip of the index finger should touch the side of the low 'E' string, to prevent it from sounding.

To test your octave muting ability, play the next example (Ex.29). Make sure to use alternate strumming strokes during the sixteenth note groups of the second bar.

Example 29 - Octave Muting Exercise   CD 29

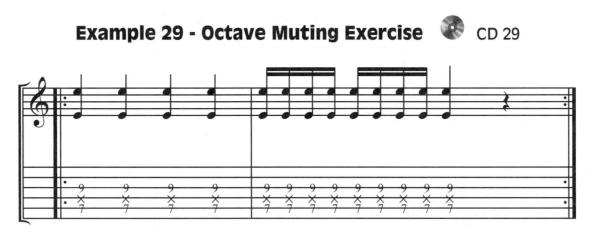

If you can hear anything ringing other than the E note on the 7th fret of the 'A' string and the E note on the 9th fret of the 'G' string, you're not applying the proper muting technique, and you'll need to reconfigure your fingers until the unnecessary strings are silenced.

To test your octave muting technique further, you should practice playing scales using octaves along the 'A' and 'G' strings. Try this C Major scale using octaves to give this muting technique a good workout (Ex.30).

Example 30 - C Major Scale Using Octaves   CD 30

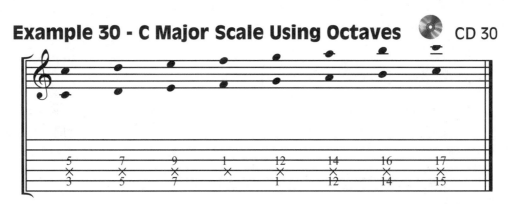

This type of octave movement along the strings is commonplace for many guitarists and has been used by Rock legends such as Jimi Hendrix and Eddie Van Halen to Jazz legends such as Wes Montgomery and Pat Metheny.

Modern Rock and Punk bands have adopted the use of octaves into their music as well, including the Pop-Punk sound of groups like Green Day, Blink 182, and Sum 41, who commonly use this transparent "chord" in many of their tunes, normally found during song intros or musical interludes.

To practice moving the octave shape to different sets of strings, play the next example (Ex.31), which moves the octave shape from the 'A' and 'G' strings, to the low 'E' and 'D' strings.

Example 31 - Octave "Shifting" Exercise CD 31

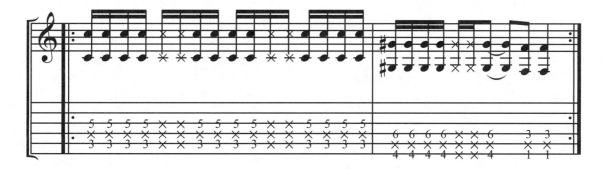

If the octave you're performing is located on the 'D' and 'B' strings or the 'G' and high 'E' strings, this will require you to use a combination of frethand thumb and finger muting. Study the next example and photo to see how to properly mute these situations (Ex.32).

Example 32 - Muting An Octave On The D And B Strings CD 32

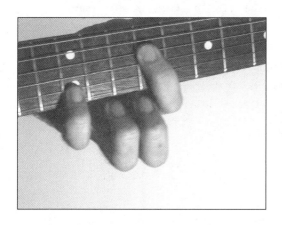
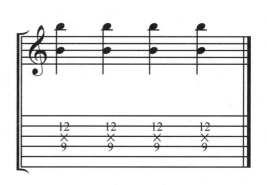

Mute the high 'E' string with the underside of the pinky finger, the 'G' with the underside of the index finger, and the thumb should mute the 'A' and low 'E' strings.

Muting this octave shape correctly is noticeably more difficult than the previous octave shape. The reason behind this revolves around an underdeveloped frethand pinky, which will give many beginning to intermediate guitarists some trouble at first.

The next octave muting situation is a common Jazz style that has been developed and performed by countless Jazz guitarists (Ex.33), which is the use of strummed octaves using the pickhand thumb, instead of using a pick. This creates a nice warm tone that many Jazz players prefer.

Example 33 - Jazz Octave Playing CD 33

String "Raking"

This percussive muted picking technique involves frethand muting and commonly found in the playing of guitar legends such as B.B. King, Stevie Ray Vaughn, and Eddie Van Halen. The result of using this technique delivers an interesting "raked" sound while proceeding into a fretted note, usually "raking" into the B or high 'E' string.

Use the frethand thumb to mute the wound strings, as the tip of the index finger can mute the 'G' string. As each note is picked, drag (or "rake") your pick across the muted strings until you've reached the targeted string/note you want to sound. Unused frethand fingers and the thumb should silence strings that are not being used.

To begin, play through this raking example, which will give you an opportunity to see, hear, and perform string "rakes" along the 'B' string (Ex.34).

Example 34 - String "Rakes" CD 34

Once you are comfortable with the first "raked" example (Ex.34), you should play around with this B.B. King flavored Blues lick, featuring muted "rakes" into notes on the 'B' and high 'E' strings (Ex.35).

Example 35 - BB King Style String "Rakes"　CD 35

When you're comfortable playing this example (Ex.35), you should try "raking" into other notes on different sets of strings, as this technique is common in a variety of musical styles and situations.

To give your string "rake" muting technique a test, play the next example (Ex.36), which will help you refine your muting control and give you an exercise to practice string "raking".

Example 36 - String "Raking" Exercise　CD 36

While playing through this exercise (Ex.36), be sure the only notes that are audible are the fretted notes that are indicated, the 'X's are the "raked" strings and should only generate a percussive sound.

As this exercise moves from string-to-string the muting technique being used will have to move with it. This common occurrence happens when you have to mute across multiple strings.

Tremolo Picking And Muting

Tremolo picking is a common picking technique that countless guitarists have used over the years. It involves rapidly plucking a chord or single note as rapidly and accurately as possible. Legendary tremolo pickers, such as Eddie Van Halen, Al Di Meola, and Dick Dale have refined this technique to a science, and each use a similar muting technique when performing it on their guitar.

To begin using this technique, play this tremolo strumming exercise (Ex.37) using the same sequence of Asus2 chord mutations shown in Example 16.

Example 37 - Tremolo Strumming/Muting CD 37

For this exercise, be sure to use the frethand thumb to mute the low 'E' string as you move the Asus2 chord shape around the fretboard in this exercise (Ex.37).

Once you're comfortable muting a chord sequence when tremolo picking, it's time to tackle single note tremolo picking, which is a little more involved. The trick behind properly muting a tremolo picking lick or run lies solely on the frethand, as the picking hand will be occupied playing the rapid alternate picking strokes.

For example, if you're tremolo picking on the 'G' string, the frethand thumb should mute the low 'E' and 'A' strings, while individual fingers from the frethand can dampen strings with the underside portion wherever applicable or possible.

The next example is a great place to begin muting tremolo picked phrases and licks (Ex.38).

Example 38 - Tremolo Picking/Muting Exercise CD 38

Chapter 3 – *Pickhand Muting Techniques*

Muting the strings of the guitar using the pickhand is every bit as common as frethand muting, as legions of guitarists from various styles of music use pickhand muting in some form. The most common techniques include the pickhand smother, palm muting (dampening), the "string silencer" technique, string isolation, and "hybrid" picking.

"Pickhand Smother" Technique

The first pickhand technique that you should experiment with is called the "pickhand smother", similar to the "frethand smother" technique that was demonstrated in the previous chapter. As the name would suggest, the "pickhand smother" involves firmly placing the side of the pickhand on the strings. The pickhand placement doesn't really matter, as the desired effect prevents all of the strings from ringing or sounding.

Carefully study the photograph below, which visually demonstrates the proper pickhand placement for the "pickhand smother" technique.

When applying this technique, it's important to stress the fact that you need to prevent any of the strings from ringing when they are plucked.

Example 39 - "Pickhand Smother" Exercise   CD 39

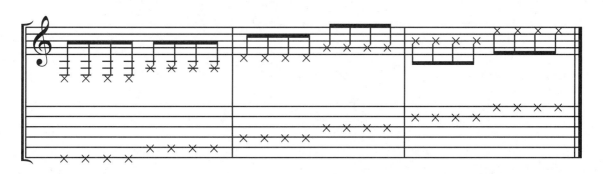

As you can see, this exercise (Ex.39) is the exact opposite of Example 1, which was a "frethand smother" exercise in the previous chapter. This is a great way to develop pickhand muting technique, as this exercise requires to successfully mute the strings using the pickhand on all six strings of the guitar.

Palm Muting Technique

Once you're comfortable applying the "pickhand smother" technique, begin exploring the various facets of palm muting. Palm muting is similar in feel to the "pickhand smother" application, as it involves placing the side of the pickhand on the strings, but the result is quite different.

The secret with this technique is the pickhand placement on the strings. The side of the pickand palm should lightly come into contact with the strings as close to the bridge as possible. Study the visual demonstration with the photos below to show you the proper pickhand placement for palm muting.

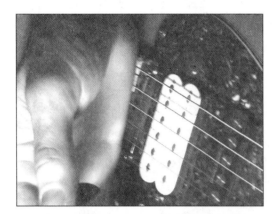 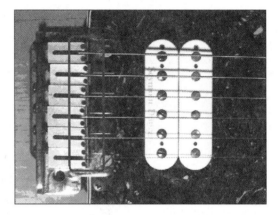

Palm muting (a.k.a. string dampening) produces a mellow and dulled sound compared to allowing the strings to ring openly, a very popular technique for countless guitarists in every imaginable style of music. Everyone from Blues guitar pioneers to Heavy Metal heroes have used palm muting in their music.

To begin using this technique, practice the next example (Ex.40), which is a useful exercise for developing palm muting skill on the low 'E' string in a Hard Rock/Metal vein.

Example 40 - Hard Rock Palm Muting   CD 40

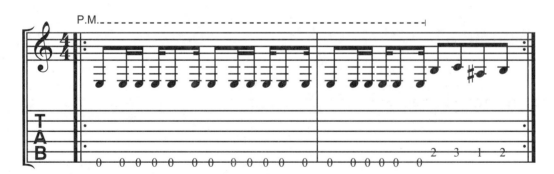

This exercise is very similar to countless Hard Rock and Metal guitar riffs. Groups such as White Zombie, Tool, and System Of A Down have played riffs like this in their music. Be sure to allow the low 'E' to ring slightly for this example (Ex.40), placing the side of the pickhand on the bridge, precisely where the strings leave the bridge of the guitar.

28

Palm muting is not only reserved for Metal and Rock guitarists, as this technique has been popular in various styles of music for quite some time. Countless Blues guitar legends have incorporated palm muting into their rhythm playing, influencing generations of Blues, Rock, and Country guitarists in the process.

Play through this common 12-bar Blues rhythm in the key of D (Ex.41), and listen to the CD carefully to hear this rhythm played with the palm muting technique. *Palm mute everything except the last bar.*

Example 41 - Palm Muted 12 Bar Blues In D CD 41

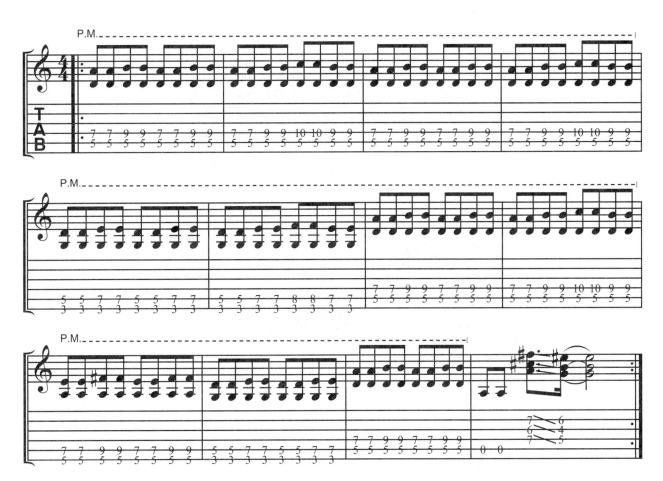

The tonal character that this technique produces is highly desired by many Blues, Rock, Country, and Metal guitarists. Palm Muting has been featured so much in fact, that many guitarists commonly take this technique for granted, once the "feel" and precise hand placement have become second nature.

The "String Silencer" Technique

The "string silencer" technique is useful in many playing situations on the guitar, such as playing chords, single-note patterns, riffs on the lower (wound) strings, trills, power chords, string bending, vibrato, etc…

The pinky and third fingers of the pickhand can come in contact with the 'B' and high 'E' strings, effectively muting these strings until they are needed or used again. While this technique might be uncomfortable to use while performing intricate strumming patterns or alternate picking, it's useful nonetheless and should be explored if you have trouble keeping the 'B' and high 'E' strings silent while playing.

Study the photo below to investigate how to apply the "string silencer" technique.

With the fingers firmly planted on these strings, they will be unplayable until the pickhand fingers are removed from the strings. This technique will prove very useful for efficiently muting string bending, which will be covered in the next chapter.

String Isolation

Isolating a string on the guitar is very similar to applying the "string silencer" technique, the difference lies in allowing one string of the guitar to be manipulated using legato (hammer-ons or pull-offs), slides, or trills.

To begin, play around with this common Blues guitar riff, using a rapidly executed trill with the open 'D' string (Ex. 42).

Example 42 - String Isolation With Trills CD 42

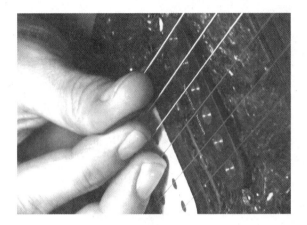

The string isolation technique involves surrounding the 'D' string using the pickhand, muting the low 'E' and 'A' strings with palm muting. The pickhand middle finger should come into direct contact with the 'G' string (using the "string silencer" technique), which will successfully mute all of the neighboring strings.

The next example of using string isolation incorporates a common open string lick using pull-offs on the 'B' string (Ex.43). The pickhand should apply palm muting to the bass (wound) strings, while surrounding the 'G' and high 'E' strings with the thumb and index finger.

Example 43 - String Isolation Open String Lick CD 43

Heavy Metal guitar heroes Randy Rhoads (Ozzy Osbourne) and Kirk Hammett (Metallica) played licks similar to this, relying on the string isolation muting technique for countless guitar solos and fills.

Muting Slides

The string isolation technique is also useful when needing to perform long slides along one string and keep everything controlled and muted. Play around with the next example (Ex.44), a useful sliding exercise to develop string isolation using an A Major scale on one string.

Example 44 - String Isolation Sliding Exercise 🔘 CD 44

During these exercises (Ex.42-44) you may "palm" the pick with the pickhand, picking the first note only, then apply string isolation around the neighboring strings to keep things quiet and muted. If you are unsure how to "palm" the pick, study the following information about incorporating this useful technique into your playing.

"Pick Palming"

"Palming" the guitar pick when applying string isolation is quite common, as this "magic trick" might take years of patient practice to perfect. Whenever you want to use the pickhand fingers while holding a pick, you may "palm" the pick in your cupped hand, or roll the pickhand index finger to hold the pick in the crease of the first knuckle, freeing the thumb and middle finger to fingerpick or mute the strings at will.

To visually see what the two most common "pick palming" techniques look like, examine the photos below for an accurate display of where you can "hide" the pick when you want to use fingers instead of the pick.

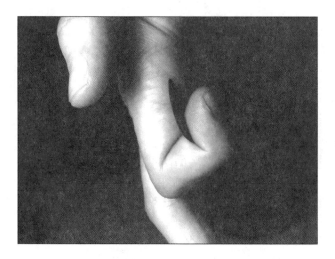
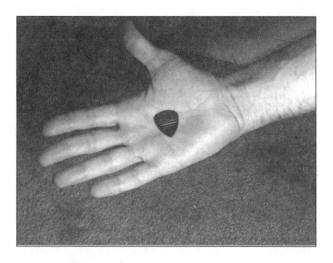

This technique is great for situations where you want to play with the fingers for a moment, only to need the pick again for strumming or alternate picking duty in a later section of a song or exercise.

"Hybrid" Picking

Another common technique that requires a skillful pickhand muting technique is called "hybrid" picking, where a plectrum and an additional pickhand finger attack the strings for an interesting sounding effect. This type of picking is common in Rock, Blues, and Country music, and has been featured in numerous songs throughout the years.

The trick behind "hybrid" picking lies in holding the pick normally with the pickhand thumb and index finger, while the pickhand middle or third finger plucks a different string.

To help you visually see what the pickhand should look like when utilizing this technique, study the following photo to see how the pickhand should be positioned.

The next example is a basic "hybrid" picking example to give your ears and fingers a chance to get comfortable with this technique (Ex.45).

Example 45 - "Hybrid" Picking Lick   CD 45

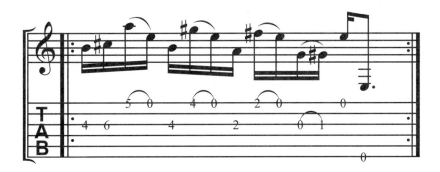

Proper pickhand muting is crucial when using the "hybrid" picking technique, as this example (Ex.45) indicates. The pickhand palm should employ a certain level of palm muting on the wound strings, while the "hybrid" middle finger plucks the high 'E' string whenever a new fretted note is played.

Practice this "tremolo hybrid" picking lick, which is very common in Blues and Country music (Ex.46). Guitarists as wide ranging from Willie Nelson to Robben Ford have explored this "hybrid" picking idea.

Example 46 - "Tremolo Hybrid" Picking Lick CD 46

Once you have the previous lick under your belt (Ex.47), you should practice another version of "hybrid" picking, featuring a "roll" technique commonly associated with fingerpicking a banjo.

The next "hybrid" picking lick features a plectrum plucked single note on the 'G' string, while the pickhand middle and third fingers "roll" forward, fingerpicking the 'B' and high 'E' string to give this lick a banjo flavored sound (Ex.47).

Example 47 - "Banjo Hybrid" Picking Lick CD 47

As you explore muting techniques with various playing techniques, you'll discover that for every playing technique performed on the guitar, a muting technique must be applied to keep things controlled and properly muted.

"Mutola" Technique

Fusion guitar master Al Di Meola has a pickhand muting technique named after him, as many of his fans have been trying for decades to incorporate his unique muting approach into their playing.

The "Mutola" technique involves placing an accurate palm muting technique with the pickhand and playing single-note runs and licks with the mute applied throughout. Although this technique is similar to regular palm muting, the "Mutola" technique barely allows the strings to ring as notes are sounded.

Al Di Meola is a true guitar master, and his blazingly fast picking runs are normally accompanied with this percussive muting technique.

To have a better understanding of this technique, listen to the audio CD demonstration carefully and try to emulate what you've heard when practicing the following exercise (Ex.48). Remember to use the pickhand smother technique with this single-note DiMeola inspired phrase.

Example 48 - "Mutola" Muting Exercise 🔘 CD 48

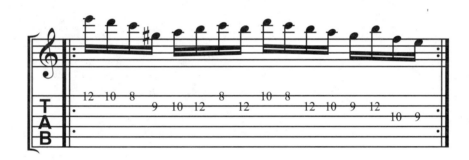

Once you have a feel for this palm muting technique shown Example 48, play through this advanced Al Di Meola style muted picking workout (Ex.49).

Example 49 - "Mutola" Muting Exercise #2 🔘 CD 49

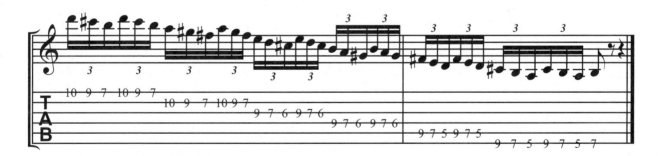

Influential Al Di Meola compositions such as 'Race With The Devil On Spanish Highway', 'The Wizard', and 'Short Tales Of The Black Forest' prove that Al Di Meola's not only a masterful musician, he's also unbelievably gifted at muting the strings of the guitar.

Chapter 4 – *Combining Muting Techniques*

Now that you've spent some time practicing frethand and pickhand muting techniques individually, you should begin combining these techniques together, which will allow you to properly mute more advanced playing situations, including string bending, "chicken" picking, legato phrasing, and pickhand tapping.

"Combination Smother"

To begin learning about combination muting, start with applying both the fretboard and pickhand "smother" techniques, insuring that the strings of the guitar will not sound, regardless of what is plucked or strummed. This technique is called the "combination smother" and is useful in a number of playing situations. Examine the photos below to visually see what "combination muting" involves.

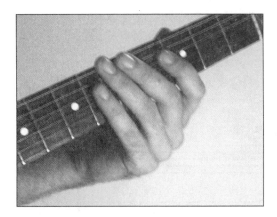
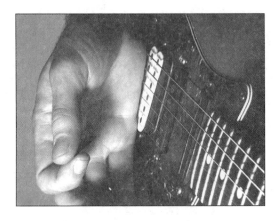

Once you have performed something on the guitar, you should make it a habit to completely silence the strings once you are finished. Dampen the strings using a combination of the "pickhand smother" and the "frethand smother" techniques, accurately silencing all of the strings.

Practice the following exercise to establish and refine using this muting technique (Ex.50).

Example 50 - "Combination Smother" Exercise CD 50

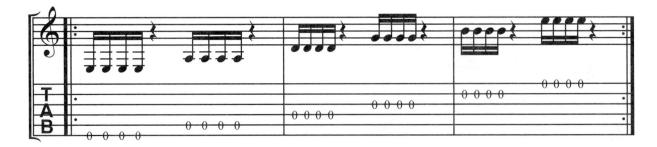

To properly perform and mute this exercise (Ex.50), you should be certain that each individual open string is silenced before moving to the next open string.

Do not let the strings ring open into one another.

To further your development when using the "combination smother" muting technique, play around with this power chord exercise, which forces you to mute the strings after each chord is strummed (Ex.51).

Example 51 - "Combination Smother" Exercise CD 51

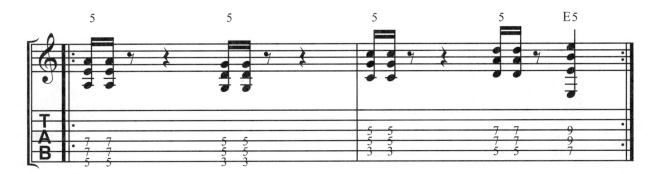

This type of muting is very common in the modern forms of Rock and Punk music, commonly used by groups such as Green Day, Blink 182, and Sum 41. As soon as the chord is sounded, mute the strings completely using a combination of frethand and pickhand muting. Listen to the CD carefully to hear how this example (Ex.52) is supposed to sound.

String Bending And Muting

Bending the strings of the guitar can be a noisy situation if the strings aren't muted properly, as this technique might produce unwanted string noise when the unused strings come into contact with the frethand fingers or with the string that is getting pushed around.

To properly mute bent notes and licks, you should use a combination of pickhand and frethand muting. Study the following suggestions to help make your bending licks and phrases sound cleaner and more professional.

1. Use multiple frethand fingers for most bending licks and phrases.
   (Try to use at least two fingers when bending a treble string!)
2. Pickhand palm muting should be employed on the wound strings in most bending situations using the treble strings.
3. The pickhand "string silencer" technique is useful for quieting the 'B' and high 'E' strings when they aren't used during wound string bends.
4. The underside of the frethand index finger can mute strings behind it, such as muting the 'B' and high 'E' strings if you're bending on the 'G' string.
5. The frethand thumb can act as insurance to silence the wound strings, namely the low 'E' and 'A' strings for bending licks on the 'G', 'B', or high 'E' strings.

Once you've reviewed these bending guidelines, continue with some actual bending situations where combination muting must be employed to guarantee accurate string muting for bending, and additional string noise is kept to a minimum.

Study the following example and photos to help you understand how to properly mute string bending on the guitar (Ex.52).

Example 52 - Muted String Bend CD 52

 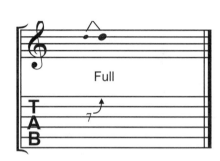 

The muting technique that you use should remain the same, no matter how far you are bending (whole step, ½ step, ¼ step, etc…). Bending notes on different strings will create slightly different muting situations, but overall the technique should be the same.

Another bending situation that is quite common is called a bend and release, where a note is raised and then released back to the original (non-bent) note.

Play through and listen carefully to the CD for the next example (Ex.53), demonstrating a common bend and release.

Example 53 - Muted Bend And Release CD 53

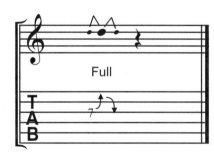

For this situation (Ex.53), make sure that the frethand thumb is keeping a few of the wound strings from sounding (at least the low 'E'), but be careful not to accidentally sound the 'A' or 'D' string during the release section of the bend.

The trick here is to keep unwanted strings from ringing during the release portion of the bend using the "string silencer" technique with the pickhand, while also using palm muting and/or frethand thumb muting for the wound strings.

To help give your muting technique more practice with bending, play around with this Rock/ Blues lick, featuring a bend and release on a different string (the high 'E'), performed in a different position on the neck (Ex.54).

Example 54 - Muted Bend And Release Lick CD 54

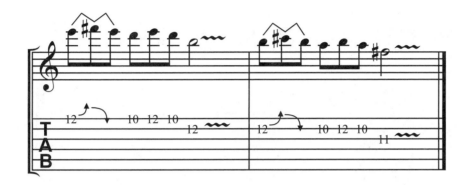

Another common type of bending using two barred notes is called double-stop bending. This bending technique authentically produces the sound of a pedal-steel guitar, commonly found in Country and Blues based music.

Play around with this "Country-fied" bending lick (Ex.55), which uses a clever combination of frethand and pickhand muting. Use pickhand palm muting technique for the unused low 'E' and 'A' strings. The tip of the frethand index finger should gently come in contact with the 'D' string.

Example 55 - Muted "Pedal Steel" Bending Lick CD 55

This type of bending is common for Country guitarists to use, such as Nashville session-ace Brent Mason, Country guitar legend Albert Lee, and the amazing Jerry Donahue from the Hellecasters. Each of these players have redefined this type of bending, creating a mixture of traditional guitar bending sounds and pedal-steel guitar licks.

Another interesting Country idea that has "crossed-over" into Rock and Blues guitar playing is called "chicken" picking, and has been used by everyone from Zakk Wylde to Vince Gill. This bending technique and the required muting technique are unusual at first, but well worth the effort.

This lick is a common "chicken" picking affair, requiring the use of pickhand fingers to pluck "or cluck" the 'G' string after it's raised a whole step (Ex.56).

Example 56 - "Chicken" Picking Lick CD 56

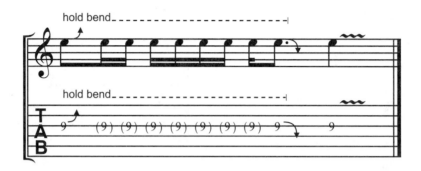

After a sequence of "plucks", release the bend gradually, muting the strings around the 'G' using a combination of frethand "smothers" and pickhand palm muting. String isolation muting may also be necessary if muting problem occur when attempting to play this lick (Ex.56).

For bending situations on the wound strings, you can utilize a combination of the "string silencer" technique and palm muting with the pickhand, while using the underside of the frethand index finger or side of the thumb to clean up bending licks on the lower strings.

Play through this typical Rock sounding riff, featuring a common bend on the low 'E' string mixed with some open position power chords (Ex.57).

Example 57 - Common Muted Rock Riff CD 57

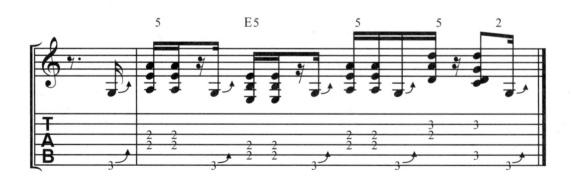

Riffs such as this have been very common in Rock music, including classic songs such as 'Same Old Song And Dance' by Aerosmith and 'Living Loving Maid' by Led Zeppelin.

Legato Phrasing And Muting

The use of legato by guitarists is very common, but for many beginning to intermediate guitarists a considerable amount string noise occurs when using this technique. Proper string muting techniques must be applied before a clean performance using legato can be attained.

Play through this common open-position legato move, using a simple D Major-Dsus4-Dsus2 chord sequence (Ex.58).

Example 58 - D Major Chord Legato   CD 58

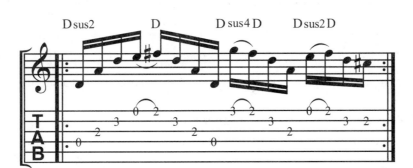

This type of playing is very common for acoustic Rock and Folk guitarists, such as Bob Dylan, James Taylor, and Neil Young, and has been used in numerous songs from various musical genres. Muting this example (Ex.58) should be quite easy, as the legato movement occurs solely on the high 'E' string. Just be sure to palm mute with the pickhand keeping the low 'E' and 'A' strings quiet.

Another common open-position legato move uses pull-offs to open strings, similar to what was shown in Example 43. Licks such as this have been used on countless recordings, including 'Crazy Train' by Ozzy Osbourne, 'Love Song' by Tesla, 'The Middle' by Jimmy Eat World, and 'I Know A Little' by Lynyrd Skynyrd (Ex.59).

Example 59 - Open Position Pull-Off Lick   CD 59

The secret behind keeping this lick muted properly lies in using the "string silencer" technique for the 'B' and high 'E' strings, while the pickhand palm mutes the wound strings, and the underside of the frethand fingers mute as the pattern moves across the strings.

For a fretted variation of Ex.59 try the next muted legato lick, a pattern popularized by guitarists such as Eddie Van Halen, Jeff Beck, and Brian Setzer (Ex.60).

Example 60 - Muted Rock Legato Lick CD 60

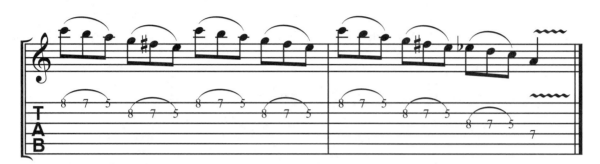

For this example (Ex.60), you'll have to mute the wound strings using the pickhand palm muting technique as the underside of the frethand index finger mutes from string to string.

Once you have developed a "feel" for muting when using legato, play through the next exercise to help develop your legato muting technique on every string (Ex.61).

Example 61 - Muted Legato Exercise CD 61

(Example 61 cont.)

"Finger Rolling"

The "rolling" finger technique is useful for handling double-stop licks and sequences on the guitar. In particular, certain Penatonic scale fingerings and licks require the use of this finger muting technique for the cleanest possible execution and delivery.

To begin, play through this A Minor Pentatonic scale using "finger" rolls as you move from string-to-string (Ex.62).

Example 62 - Finger "Rolling" Technique CD 62

The basic finger "rolling" technique uses the individual knuckles of the frethand, as the finger "bends" to accommodate two notes on adjacent strings, but only one note on each string should sound at a time.

Once you have the basic technique of finger "rolling" down, you will be able to incorporate intricate finger movements and phrases into your fills and solos.

Play around with this Rock/Blues lick that features some intense finger "rolling" (Ex.63).

Example 63 - Finger "Rolling" Blues-Rock Lick CD 63

Pickhand Tapping And Muting

Guitar legend Eddie Van Halen helped the world discover pickhand tapping (a.k.a. right-hand tapping) in the late 1970s, thanks in part to his monumental guitar moments, such as 'Eruption' and 'Spanish Fly'. While many guitarists are now familiar with pickhand tapping, many are confused about how to properly mute the strings while the pickhand performs tapped runs and licks.

The secret lies in using the "palming" technique to free the index finger for tapped phrases, and the pickhand will help mute unwanted or unused strings when tapping. The photo below will help you visually witness how to successfully mute pickhand tapping phrases and licks.

You should notice that the pickhand thumb is resting against the low 'E' string, successfully muting this string for tapped phrases. The area on the side of the pickhand palm just above the wrist is placed strategically on idle strings to assist in keeping everything muted and silent.

Play around with this basic tapping lick, which will give you an opportunity to adjust your pickhand for a proper muting technique when tapping (Ex.64). Aim for muting everything surrounding the B string as you play this lick, using parts of both of your hands to dampen and mute the unwanted strings.

Example 64 - Pickhand Tapping Lick  CD 64

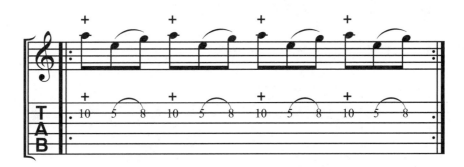

Once you are comfortable muting the strings with tapping licks such as this, you should practice this cliché Van Halen tapping lick, which involves moving the frethand portion of Example 64 (Ex.65).

Example 65 - Van Halen Inspired Tapping Lick CD 65

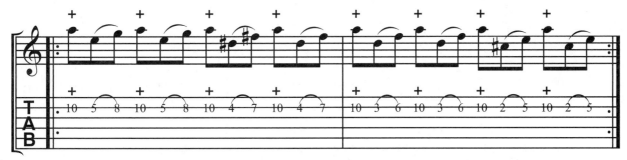

To give your pickhand tapping technique and muting a workout, play through this stretchy tapping lick in the style of classic Van Halen tapping moments, such as 'Hot For Teacher' and 'Spanish Fly' (Ex. 66).

Example 66 - Advanced Van Halen Tapping Lick  CD 66

Play through this tapping idea made popular by guitarists such as Eddie Van Halen, Michael Hedges, and Joe Satriani (Ex. 67).

Example 67 - Advanced Two-Handed Tapping CD 67

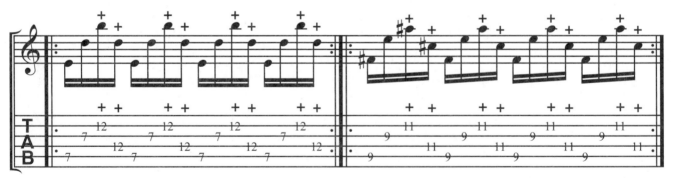

"Overhand" Muting

"Overhand" muting is an uncommon occurrence in most guitar circles, but many "flashy" Rock guitarists pull this trick out to amaze and impress their audience. Players such as Eddie Van Halen, Steve Vai, Joe Satriani, and Buckethead have all used this technique in one form or another.

The secret behind this "trick" involves placing the pickhand behind the frethand on the fretboard to mute and/or fret the strings, as the frethand uses hammer-ons or pull-offs on a higher region of the fretboard. If you're muting with this technique, you should lightly place the pickhand across the strings to mute them behind the frethand, if you're fretting behind the frethand, you can position you pickhand fingers to perform fretting and muting simultaneously.

The easiest way to understand how to mute this technique is to study the next example (Ex.68), giving you an opportunity to hear, read, and investigate how to use this playing technique. For this lick, you'll want to fret the 5th fret on the G string with the pickhand behind the frethand, while using pull-offs with the frethand.

Example 68 – "Overhand" Fretting Technique CD 68

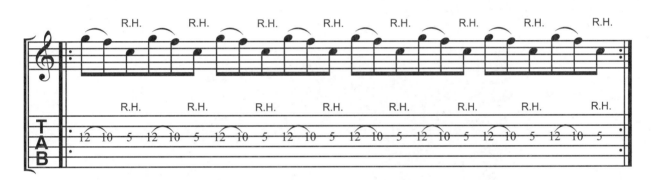

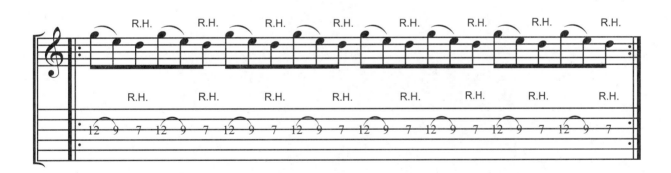

Now that you have the basic technique, play around with this "overhand" muting lick, similar to patterns used by Joe Satriani on songs such as 'Mystical Potato Head Groove Thing' and 'Power Cosmic' (Ex.69).

Example 69 - "Overhand" Satriani Muting Technique CD 69

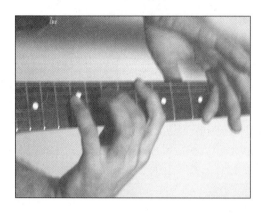 

Studying the photo above will help you visually understand how to mute the previous two examples (#68-69). These are advanced applications of muting the guitar, so don't feel discouraged or worried if you're having trouble reproducing what is heard on the CD.

Muting Finale

This final exercise utilizes many of the muting techniques and situations that were discussed in this book, in one complete exercise. These techniques include palm muting, the "string silencer" technique, frethand "smothering", finger "rolling", and frethand thumb muting.

This exercise is a great picking workout in addition to being a great way to check your muting technique on every string on the guitar (Ex.70).

Example 70 - E Major Muting Exercise   CD 70

More Great Guitar Books from Centerstream...

More Great Guitar Books from Centerstream...

You, learning with **Centerstream** Books and DVD's.

Without.